Lightness and Darkness Cannot Mix

LIGHTNESS AND DARKNESS CANNOT MIX

Open Your Spiritual Eye

SHEELA R. WILEY

XULON PRESS

Xulon Press
2301 Lucien Way #415
Maitland, FL 32751
407.339.4217
www.xulonpress.com

© 2021 by Sheela R. Wiley
Foreword by Linda L. Daniels

All rights reserved solely by the author. The author guarantees all contents are original and do not infringe upon the legal rights of any other person or work. No part of this book may be reproduced in any form without the permission of the author. The views expressed in this book are not necessarily those of the publisher.

Due to the changing nature of the Internet, if there are any web addresses, links, or URLs included in this manuscript, these may have been altered and may no longer be accessible. The views and opinions shared in this book belong solely to the author and do not necessarily reflect those of the publisher. The publisher therefore disclaims responsibility for the views or opinions expressed within the work.

Unless otherwise indicated, Scripture quotations taken from the King James Version (KJV)–*public domain.*

Paperback ISBN-13: 978-1-6628-3130-0
Ebook ISBN-13: 978-1-6628-3131-7

Dedication

To my Mommy dearest and Father who raised me up in admiration and fear of the Lord. I love my parents so much. I love the fact that they instilled prayer and the Word of God in me. They taught me to seek God for myself.

Table of Contents

Acknowledgements ix
Foreword xi
Introduction xiii
Preface xv

Chapter 1
Unanticipated and Unplanned Pleasures 1
   I'd just lost my dad 1
   My marriage was at a co-existing stage 3

Chapter 2
Hold Your Head Up -. 7
   The Affair – The Luring 7
   The Affair – Love Bombing 12
   The Affair – The Discard 25
   The Affair –The Trickery 28
   The Self Pity 30

Chapter 3
I'm a Survivor–Ran from a Narc 33
   Verbal Abuse–Emotional 33
   Physical Abuse -. 34
   Mental abuse - 35

Chapter 4
Shhh....keep this between you and me 39

Chapter 5
True Deliverance–True Repentance................. 41

Chapter 6
Which would you choose, Hell on earth for a season or Hell with the devil for an eternity?........ 45

Chapter 7
Do you Fear the Lord?............................47

Chapter 8
Have you been turned over to reprobate? 49

Chapter 9
Just when you thought everything was alright, you allowed the devil to step back in................59

Chapter 10
Get thee behind me Satan!....................... 61
    How did I Come to meet the Narcissists, anyway? Since when did ministry become about us and no longer about God?.............62

Chapter 11
The Importance of having a father in your life-....... 71

Chapter 12
You don't know the cost of my oil - 73

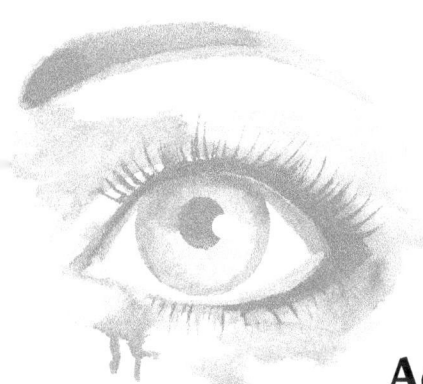

Acknowledgements

I would like to thank my prayer warriors. These women relentlessly helped to hold me up when I no longer felt any hope in life. Please understand: it is one thing to be trampled and left for dead outside of the church; but when you are trampled and left for dead inside of the church, it is a very hurtful thing. These ladies fasted and intervened before God for me to not give up on my faith and love for Him. I want to thank my true friends who I called whenever I needed to talk and release my sharp pain. They did not judge me. They allowed me to cry and vent.

Foreword

This author is one of the most respected, influential prayer warrior and intercessor for other prayer partners who faithfully seek God. Her anointing and faith in Him allowed her experience to endure the heartless and ungodly actions of the church. Her courage and integrity for writing this book as an intercessory prayer leader, will reveal and assure readers they can release and restore the quality of life to those who trust and seek God.

Linda L. Daniels

Introduction

*I*s there such a thing as narcissistic abuse? Is it possible for narcissistic abuse to come through church leaders, such as pastors, prophets and teachers? The answer to both of those questions is absolutely, yes! Never would I have thought that I would experience such behavior in my place of worship with like-minded believers. Church, as I know it is a hospital. It is a place where you go to find refuge, peace and hope. Not so at this place. The best description of this church was more like a "front" where behind closed doors was a demonic cult. A front is when you are using a median to camouflage your true intent. Have you ever heard of the transferring of spirits? Are you familiar with Jezebel, Leviathan and Ahab? Well, those are a few of the many demonic spirits that were in operation at this cult. Because I am a prophetic intercessor, the Holy Ghost revealed so much to me about what was going on behind the scenes. That place was infested with the spirit of Jezebel, Leviathan and Ahab. I was a prayer warrior, so I really never thought that those spirits could transfer onto me, but guess what? Life happens and when it does, the devil waits for a time to enter into your temple. This is what happened to me and suddenly my light turned into darkness. Over time, while attending this cult, after having the adulterous relationship with pastor Narc, instead of excitedly running through the church doors, I soon began crying before entering. The agony of just thinking about approaching that place made me anxious; and the Word of God says to be anxious for nothing. Anxiety is not of God. I was in so much pain, I became numb to life. As you read, I will share with you what caused me to fall into the trap of the narcissist; and then further go into detail about how that narcissistic relationship looked and felt. Lightness and Darkness Cannot Mix - Open Your Spiritual Eye -

Luke 11:34-35

> [34] *"The eye is the lamp of your body; when your eye is clear, your whole body also is full of light; but when it is bad, your body also is full of darkness.* [35] *Then watch out that the light in you is not darkness."*

Preface

This book was written to bring awareness to how narcissistic abuse in church leaders brings corruption within the body of Christ. Narcissism, is a personality disorder that is often times developed because of a traumatic event that occurred in the narcissists' life during their adolescent years. Narcissists are known to be sexual predators, murders, child abusers. Their main characteristics are the need to control, blame others and self-centeredness. This book is based upon my real life story. I ran into the arms of a narcissistic pastor. Yes, it sounds really degrading doesn't it? I sound like a harlot. In the beginning, I was really indecisive about sharing my story with the world; but this was too devastating and traumatizing to keep to myself. I was led by the Holy Spirit to share my story. I do not know if there are other books that discuss the desire to do God's will while feeling rejected by the highest church members — the church officials. In the scriptures, the Word of God tells us that He is the head of the body (the church) and we worship and honor only Him and give Him glory in all things.

Perhaps you've come face to face with a narcissist and really did not know it? My prayer is as you read this, that you are not judgmental; but you become enlightened and truly understand that this is real. Narcissistic abuse is real.

There is a pattern that a narcissist holds true to when they are involved in relationships. The stages are: idealize, devalue, and discard. In some parts of this book, you may want to cover your eyes and drop your lip. Then in others, you may think, "Shame on you". Whatever your response, know that this is my story and I chose to tell the truth in the hope that someone else may receive the deliverance and freedom that he/she so desperately needs. I believe this book will touch the heart of one who has experienced such turmoil. My prayer is that this book will encourage you to direct your attention towards the One who truly deserves the honor and the glory in this walk of life. No one, even our pastors and ministers, should be put on a pedestal and be honored as a god. Those pastors and ministers who may have such gifts and anointing may sometimes act prideful, which is not God. They want acknowledgment, total trust and love to be cherished by all. Regardless of how good they may be, it will bring you discouragement and disillusionment.

Trusting and believing in our Lord and Savior Jesus Christ and not forgetting whose you are and belong to will be your strength and release.

I say to all, trust God and keep the faith.

Chapter 1

Unanticipated and Unplanned Pleasures

I'd just lost my dad

To everything there is a season, and a time to every purpose under the heaven: A time to be born, and a time to die; a time to plant, and a time to pluck up that which is planted; **Ecclesiastes 3:1-2**. My family was together until I was about eight years old (roughly). Once my parents split, I resided with my mom. I was daddy's little girl when my parents were still together. There was a period in my life where my dad and I really bonded well. I was a sickly child. I could not walk. Based upon my sickness and not being able to attend school, I spent a lot of time with my dad. Daddy had to carry me around. I can remember him talking to

God about me and believing God for my healing. I do not remember much about my dad but what I do remember is that he was a Reverend and he took care of his family. He was not perfect though. Thinking back on my childhood, I have grown to see that consequences have always been around. Whenever we act out of the Will of God, there will always be consequences. There is just no way around them. After becoming an adult woman, the tables with my dad flipped. Instead of him looking after me, became the caretaker. I was not his main caretaker; but I would help to try and take care of some of his business affairs. Because of his independence, he rarely allowed me to make decisions for him, even if they were the best decisions for him. As a child, although, I knew that he may not have been making the best choices, I would still try to respect his independence and honor him as my daddy. The Word of God says to, ***"Honor your father and your mother, so that you may live long in the land the Lord your god is giving you."* Exodus 20:12.** Towards the end of my dad's life he became a very lonely man, but he still wanted his independence. By this time, I was married. Daddy was extremely stubborn and once he set his mind to do or not to do something, that settled it! I'd lost my dad in July 2019. This really hurt because of the lack of time that I'd spent with him. We never really got to know each other during my adolescent years. He did not even walk me down the aisle on my wedding day. A lot of pain came out of knowing that I would never know much about my dad and he would never know anything else about me. Because I had never experienced the death of a close loved one before, I was really scared about how this would affect my psyche. My husband tried to be there as much as he could, but there was still a void. There was an ache that he could not fill.

My marriage was at a co-existing stage

Shortly after the death of my dad, my husband and I separated. We were just about to celebrate our five year anniversary; but I remember telling him on our anniversary day that I could not go on another year in our current state. We were not growing. The same amount of personal information that I knew about my husband year one was still the same information that I knew about him in year five. He'd given me the world, but never his heart. He never opened up to me. We did not fight. As a matter of fact, it was if we were still dating each other. He would still bring home flowers for me each week. I would have never seen this coming. I do not think that he saw it coming either. During the course of this journey, I tried several times to either show him or tell him how I really felt. I had even tried to get us marriage counseling, attend marriage conferences, etc.; but he would object to attending because he felt everything was fine. Previously, I had accepted the way things were, because I did have financial security. He did give me the world. That thought did not last, because I still needed him to fill the void of love in our relationship. Marriage is honorable before God. This is when we can freely have companionship and intimacy with our spouse and God. Joy should follow such intimacy as well God's glorification. It was also designed to take care of our aloneness.

I did not feel a true happiness in my marriage. There was a major disconnect between my husband and I. For years I tried my hardest to live out **Ephesians 5:22-33 – *"Wives, it should be no different with your husbands. Submit to them as you do to the Lord, for God has given husbands a sacred duty to lead as the Anointed leads the church and serves as the head. (the church is His body; He is her Savior.");*** but my husband was non-responsive.

I suppose you are wondering where I am going with this. Well, in both of the cases with my husband and the death of my dad, which occurred simultaneously, there was a void that I so deeply desired to have filled. That void was love, affirmation and attention.

My unanticipated and unplanned pleasure with a narcissist were birthed as a result. What I am about to share with you has forever changed my life. My prayer is that as you are reading and if you are able to identify or see yourself in this, just know that you are not alone. For me, I only wanted God. I only wanted to do what I do best, which is HELP OTHERS! Instead, I had almost lost my mind. I had almost lost my life.

Whenever you are serious about your relationship with God, the enemy will try to creep in whatever way that he can. ***"The thief comes only to steal and kill and destroy; I have come that they may have life and have it to the full."* John 10:10**. As an intercessor, you want to always stay awake. Now, because we were all born into sin, we of course are not perfect; so if things do go left in your life, do not beat yourself up, just repent and try again. ***"There is therefore now no*** *condemnation to them which are in Christ Jesus, who walk not after the flesh, but after the Spirit." Romans 8:1.*

At this time, a new pastor had just started at my church. I had been attending that ministry for five years. Things were rough for me there. The warfare that occurred in my life due to praying for my leader was significant! In other words, there was a lot of warfare. The new pastor, (who I will refer to as Pastor Narc – short for Narcissist) and I had grown close over the weeks. Here is where the irony comes into play. He was an older man. He reminded me of my dad. He displayed so much love, which is what I needed. Over a short period of time, he began showing me a plethora of attention, which if you remember, was another sign of affection that I so deeply needed. He reached out to me and asked if I would work closely with him as his Event Manager. I am the type of person who does not like disappointing anyone or telling anyone no, so I accepted. Also, I saw it as an honor to serve a man of God. Our relationship soon crossed the line. I allowed him to take advantage of me. I blamed myself for quite some time. I told myself that if I would have just not been friendly, if I would have just said no, then my marriage would be intact. I never imagined anything like this would be happening to me at the place where I fellowshipped with the people of God. Had I known what I know now, I would have run and not looked back. All the while, I thought that this man was genuine; however, he had targeted me from the very beginning and had a plan to manipulate me the entire time. I trusted this man to with whom to share my personal problems; but instead he was the DEVIL himself. I soon discovered that he was a narcissist. *"But the fearful, and unbelieving, and the abominable, and murderers, and whoremongers, and sorcerers, and idolaters, and all liars, shall have their part in the lake which burneth with fire and brimstone: which is the second death." Revelation 21:8*. A narcissist, can also be thought of as a demon. The demon spirits that a narcissist possess are the Jezebel, Leviathan and Ahab spirits. Jezebel operates under the seducing spirit. Leviathan is the king of pride. Ahab was Jezebel's husband, and he was outrightly evil. As we move on, I will point out the behaviors of Pastor Narc which allowed me to recognize the spirits with which I was dealing. Developing a soul tie with a demon is no joke. This relationship was not like any other past relationship. I was sleeping with the enemy. I am here to tell the story of how I survived.

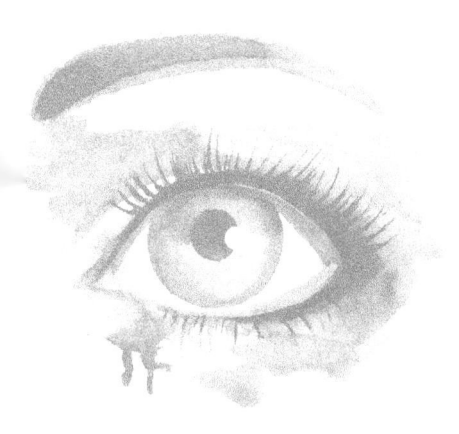

Chapter 2

Hold Your Head Up –

The Affair – The Luring

It began at the Holy Convocation – July 2019, this is a yearly event where all of the churches in this fellowship would gather in one place. It would be filled with activities and speakers the entire week. Pastor Narc came to me and introduced himself. He showed so much love to me. At that time, that was what I needed. The love that he was showing to me was how he was luring me in. He began to pique my interest. I began asking myself the question, "Who is this man who keeps paying so much attention to me?" ***"And marvel not; for Satan himself is transformed into an angel of light." 2 Corinthians 11:14***. For me, it was innocent. He reminded me of a loving father figure. We took a picture together and exchanged numbers at that time. As time went on, we would speak at service and that was the extent of it. In September, I attended an out of town event that he attended as well. He asked me for a ride back to Jacksonville; of course, with it being one of my pastors, I agreed. Before then, he had invited me to his birthday dinner. He told me that he did not have family here in Jacksonville, and we, the members of the church were his family, so of course, I would have felt bad for turning him down. During our two-hour drive back to the city, we had a pleasant conversation about the ministry that we attended. Once I arrived home, my husband told me that he did not think I should attend the birthday party because the time had grown late. I told him that I already committed; and that I could sleep after the party. He reluctantly drove us to the dinner, which was an hour away. My husband asked me why it was so important to attend the party. (My husband never asked such questions). Well, going through what we have been through, I should have listened to him and stayed home. Looking back, it was as if my husband knew something. At the dinner, we all were socializing and enjoying ourselves. My husband was even conversing, I guess because there was another military veteran there. After dinner, the group began taking pictures; my husband, of course did not participate. After a while, he began to get restless, all I knew was that he yelled across the building to me, "Let's go!!!". I was so embarrassed. I was not expecting that type of behavior from him. The next day, Pastor Narc called me to see if I was okay. He then asked if my husband hit me or if he had ever hit me and I told him no. I informed him that my husband was not a violent person. Pastor Narc further told me that he was going to call me that night and get a hotel room for us to stay in so that he could keep me safe. I thanked him and told him that was not necessary. On Sunday evening, Pastor Narc and I talked on the phone and then before we ended the conversation, he told me that he wanted to talk to me about my marriage on the following Tuesday. During our Tuesday conversation, he conducted a thorough study with me regarding my marriage, scripture references and all. He was trying to say that my husband and I were unequally yoked and he did not think I should be with my husband. He instructed me to ponder upon the scripture, **2 Corinthians 6:14 – "Do not be unequally yoked together with unbelievers. For what fellowship has righteousness with lawlessness? And what communion has light with darkness?"** He later began asking me questions about my sex life and I began to giggle because I was not used to anyone asking me about that. I had never counseled with my pastors about my marriage. As a matter of fact, at that church, I'd never confided about anything to anyone; and I should have kept it that way. He asked whether my husband and I were being intimate. He told me not to be afraid to discuss this. He then told me that I need to get the thang – thang in my life! In other words, pastor Narc was telling me that I needed to have some penis in my life! I said, "well, I guess so". He told me that I should not be embarrassed. This was discussed during our Tuesday's conversation. We got off of the phone thereafter. He reached back out to me in October 2019, I remember it was hurricane season. He first sent me a text message stating that he wanted me to work closely with him as his Event Manager. I was honored that he'd asked me, so I accepted. We then had a face-to-face lunch meeting. There we discussed in more detail my duties and expectations. As we were wrapping up our meeting, I told him that I was adopting him as my dad and he accepted and then told me that he adopted me as his daughter. This is how I viewed him. I was so excited. I felt like the void of no longer having my dad around was being filled. I felt really comfortable talking to him. I was so excited that I shared the great news with my mom, husband and the prayer team. I was even thanking God. From that point, I would complete whatever tasks the pastor put before me. I was exuberantly happy. I was finally able to be of help in ministry.

Pastor Narc called me one day as I was coming back into town. He wanted me to attend a concert with him that evening; but I'd already had plans that evening to spend time with my husband. He then tried to exercise his authority and told me that after my wifey duties, to meet him at the church. He would be calling me around 8 pm. I met him at the church and the concert was interesting. We were basically promoting the concert that he was putting on at our ministry. That evening was really eventful. We were on lockdown in the building for a while, because outside, there was a shooting, yes a gun fight! I remember making a statement – "My husband told me to begin carrying my gun on me for protection." Pastor Narc then got close to me, hugged me from behind and told me that I did not have to worry about a gun because he would protect me. Although, that was not an appropriate move that he made, he actually made me feel safe. He made me feel wanted. Once we were finally able to leave, he walked me to my car. Because he was not from Jacksonville, I called him to see if he made it out okay. He told me that he was going to grab a bite to eat. I asked him why did he not invite me. He then asked me if I wanted to dine with him and I said yes. We met at a restaurant and because it was such a nice night, I asked if we could sit on the balcony. He said that he had never been on the balcony, but he would give it a try. The ambience was so nice. I told him that I needed to call my husband because I'd already told him that I would be on my way home. Pastor Narc asked me why I had to call my husband. He also said that I told him too much. Pastor Narc told me that when I tell too much, it allows the other person to wonder. He told me how beautiful I was. He even asked the waiter if he thought that I was beautiful. He then told me that we were on a date. I was in awe. I asked him, how could we be on a date when I'm married? He told me that I deserved to be treated like the queen that I was. As hard and professional I wanted to come across, he was actually warming my heart. I hadn't felt wanted in so long. This was exactly what my heart needed. I could feel my guard going down. I told him that I felt like walking, so we drove over to the Riverwalk and began walking the path. It was such a perfect night. We began walking and talking and he put his arm around me. I felt so safe and secure in his arms. We then stopped under the light post and he leaned in and gave me a gentle, warm kiss. It was over then. One thing led to another. I'd forgotten who I was and who he was as well. We were both caught up in the moment. He was saying all the right things to lure me in more and more. I soon realized that it was not right and remembered that I was married; but I could not stop until he stopped. It was after 1 am by this time and we had to be at Sunday morning service the next morning. As I was driving home, I suddenly realized that I'd committed adultery on my husband. I felt bad but for some reason, I could not stop. It was like he brought life back into me. I felt a way that I'd never felt for any man before. It felt like black magic, if there were such a thing! This should have been a huge red flag. The demonic was in operation. I had an open door, which made me vulnerable. I was lonely in my marriage and I was grieving my dad, so I felt even lonelier. There was a lot of demonic activity going on here. In the church that pastor Narc and I attended, there were several lingering spirits. Now that I look back, I was never supposed to be there. I was lured in by the seductive spirit. The spirit that was on Pastor Narc, was the same spirit that was infesting the church. I remember after the fact, a couple of people noticed the spirit on me. If I could describe the characteristics of that spirit, it would look similar to this. You are giddy, perverse and nonchalant. You are aware of what's going on, but have no moral conscious. This is why I could cheat on my husband without any problem. I knew that it would hurt him, but all I could think about was myself.

The Affair – Love Bombing

From that point on, our affair was official. We talked and laughed every day. He was so romantic. He would send me either a romantic text or song spontaneously throughout the day. I worked from home, so it was easy for us to see each other. I made sure to return home by the time my

Lightness and Darkness Cannot Mix

husband was getting in from work. On the night of the concert, Pastor Narc introduced me to all of his friends. He would always say, "isn't she beautiful?". He had a way of making me feel special. He had a way of making me feel like I was the only woman on this green earth. After the concert ended, he gave me a kiss and a hug in the building's hallway. We then went to his office and I waited in there as he changed his clothes. He kissed me and I said, "Oh no, not in the church". He did not seem to mind. I felt like I had fallen in love in a matter of a few days. I was so happy. He made me feel so special. As time progressed, he took me golfing. He brought me into his world. I did not realize at the time that I was slowly losing myself. He would call me all throughout the night while I was home. My husband never paid attention to me anyway, so I could literally be in the other room having a conversation with Pastor Narc. My husband and Pastor Narc were like night and day. I went from 0-100 as it related to attention. He and I went from spending time together during the day before my husband got home to me spending the night practically every night of the week and weekend. Because it was so weird and I'd never done anything like this before, I began lying to my husband and told him that I was spending time with my mom. I even told my mom that if my husband called, to tell him that I was with her. I began doing things that I'd never done before; but I did not care, I was blinded by so called love. When my husband went to bed, I would set our home alarm and leave for the night. I know that he began to wonder about what I was doing. However, the month before our 5-year anniversary, I told my husband that I could not live the way that we were living anymore. Although we did not have any arguments, and he gave me the world, all I ever wanted was him. Each year was the same. We grew in years, but we never grew close together. I did not know much about him nor did he know much about me. He worked and paid attention more to his tv than me. I felt no type of connection with him. When I told him how I felt, he was frantic and said that we should go to counseling. Things began getting really quiet at home. We still spent Thanksgiving and Christmas together that year, but things were not the same. I text him one night while at church. I told him that I thought we needed to separate for a while so that I could think about things. He agreed to give me my space. I really felt bad for cheating on my husband but I could not stop. Pastor Narc was so persistent that I did not want to disappoint him. My sneaking out became just outright open. Pastor Narc and I lived together from Sunday evening to Wednesday morning every week. Of course I went home for a while each day, but I was with Pastor Narc by dusk and throughout the night. We began our courting state. He sat me down and told me that he was married but that I should not worry. I trusted him. Once again, he made me feel like his #1. Pastor Narc came to Jacksonville alone. Although he is married, his wife did not move to Jacksonville with him. Another red flag. Before I met him I used to pray a lot and belonged to certain prayer groups. Once, when I was at his house, he woke up one morning and asked me what was I doing. I told him that I was meditating on the Word and praying. He told me to shut it down and that I was doing too much. See these red flags? What does the devil do? He tries to pull you away from the things of God. I never saw him praying. He never prayed over our food. He never prayed for me. He watched tv all day and played golf. Behind closed doors, he lived a God-less life. Even when we went out, he never referred to himself as a pastor. If we were around other pastors, he would not communicate with them. He was like an odd ball. We had a few favorite restaurants and spots where we would dine after church. I loved our rendezvous. We would walk hand in hand and just laugh and joke about stuff. I even wrote him a poem exemplifying how I really felt about him. We took pictures all of the time. After about a month of love bombs, I began seeing another side of him. This is when things became crazy! He would get so angry. He would accuse me of sleeping with every man who was in attendance at our ministry. I would say to myself, "why is he accusing me so much?". I remember back in the day, if you accuse someone of doing something then you are doing it yourself. I told him that and he said it was not true. He would always ask me about my husband. He thought that my husband and I were having sex. Then he would apologize for asking me since I was still married. Pastor Narc was really jealous of my husband. For the rest of our relationship, he became extremely jealous. Things began getting really toxic. He shared a lot of personal things. He confided in me. He vented to me. Pretty much, I was his punching bag. He would make me feel sorry for him because he hadn't been paid and that he had bills past due. I began helping him pay his bills. He paid me back only once. I went from occasionally paying bills paying bills all the time.. I was doing his grocery shopping, taking care of his dry cleaning, picking up the tab (as we were always eating out) and taking care of him sexually. Our relationship really grew toxic when I would not do what he wanted. Pastor Narc began physically, emotionally and mentally abusing me. Every week, I found myself defending myself against his accusations. It became mentally draining. I was not allowed to talk to the other pastors at the ministry. I could not engage in conversation with any of the men either. If I were on my phone during church, he would ask me who was I texting. I remember leaving the sanctuary to make a few business related calls and he followed me out, acting as if he was going to his office. He was just trying to see who I was talking to. He even looked at my text messages and FB messenger on a couple of occasions to see if I was talking to any other guys. He tried his hardest to catch me doing something. We were also having heavy sex. He was an extremely horny old man. We could have just finished arguing and then end up each other's arms. We had sex in the bed, on the sofa, in the room chair, on the sink, on the dining room table, and on the car. Once we had sex, being mad at each other went out the window. He would calm down. We continued in this pattern until his son came to stay with him. During the time we were together, the more we argued, the more I realized that I'd messed up and that I no longer wanted to be with him. I began praying over him and myself, asking God to help me get out of this. I also realized at that time that he was nothing like my dad. The devil will come in whatever form he wills to deceive you and get you off track. ***2 Corinthians 11:12-15*** states, ***"12 But what I do, that I will do, that I may cut off occasion from*** *them which desire occasion; that wherein they glory, they may be found even as we.*

13 For such are false apostles, deceitful workers, transforming themselves into the apostles of Christ.

14 And no marvel; for Satan himself is transformed into an angel of light.

15 Therefore it is no great thing if his ministers also be transformed as the ministers of righteousness; whose end shall be according to their works." We will be wiped out by now.

Well, God did just that. God began to trouble the water. Although our relationship became really toxic, we would break up and get back together. He was always threatening to leave; but would come back to my home and find me. He would give me the silent treatment and then after a couple of days, he would call me back. No matter how toxic, I still loved him. The relationship was addictive. I also believe that, at the time, I would settle for any attention (whether good or bad) over no attention. Months passed and I randomly asked if he would, for once, buy me something. Cater to me, etc. He did a few times, but it came with a catch. I began learning his pattern. He thought I was not catching on but I knew. I just did not say anything. When we go to the store or the restaurants, he would act as if he had forgotten his wallet. I knew that he intentionally left it just so I could pay. I remember he told me that his mom died early because she worried too much. He went on to say that his dad lived long because he did not stress. I surmised that he was trying to get me to spend all of my money on him. I am so glad that I never shared any personal financial information with him. The Pastor Narc always had the same daily schedule but after his son moved in, I did not come over to his house much anymore. We celebrated his birthday in August, but shortly thereafter, like the next week, he and I had a really big argument. He told me that I had become stingy with my favors and that I did not want to give him money anymore. One thing about him, he would jab at me until he got his way; or if I did not buy into his foolishness, he would shut me out. Then I would call him. He would act as if he were upset with me and then I would finally give in to his demands. I noticed that he would only be happy with me when things were going his way. He was so selfish, he didn't even spend my birthday with me. He had new weekly office hours working at the church and had band rehearsal later that evening. I was fussing because I'd already reminded him that it was my birthday. He claimed that he was going to leave rehearsal early in time for us to have dinner and spend the night together. He did try to make up for it though. In September, he and I had a really big argument. We were texting back and forth during a church service one night and then the conversation went left. He got so angry with me that he told me he hated me. After the service, we met down the road from the church to talk. Well, he put on a REALLY BIG SHOW! I should have sent that production to Tyler Perry. He would not listen to my explanation. He acted as if he were crying and that I'd hurt him so bad. Then he told me he would never allow me to hurt him again. I did not understand what he was trying to do at the time. My naive self did not know that he was trying to find a reason to back off for the time being. The next day we talked, but he insisted that it was going to take a lot for him to trust me again. I began calling him and noticed that he was no longer picking up the phone. I could not reach him on FaceTime either. I thought that was odd. I was used to talking to him every day and every night. I used to be at his house the majority of the week. At church, I'd began noticing that he would sit in his car and I could always hear a female's voice coming from the phone in the car even though the windows were up. Instead of us seeing each other after church, he would say that he was hanging out with the other pastors. I began to stop calling him and once I did, he would reach out to me and ask me why he hadn't heard from me. I told him that I did not believe in chasing a man and he told me that I should since we were in this predicament because of me. So, I then tried to make another attempt to try and make things work. I purchased a sentimental gift and surprised him with it after Bible study. During Bible study, he text me a love note. Of course, I allowed him to melt my heart again. After service, I met him outside and gave him the gift. He then proceeded to tongue my ear. Man, this guy did so much to turn me on it was ridiculous! Time passed and once again he had started becoming more inconsistent. I was at his house one Saturday, I left to go to the store and walked directly back in his house. This time, I saw him looking down at his tablet and smiling. The smile was a familiar one. It was the type of smile that he used to give me in the very beginning. He put his finger up to his mouth as if he was telling me to be quiet. He then hung up the call. He asked me why I just burst in and not knock? I asked him, why I needed to knock if I was coming right back? I asked him who he was talking to and he said that he was talking to one of the other pastors' girls. He told me that they were coming over. For one, I could not understand why the other pastor would want him to talk to his girl? I then tried to look at his phone and he snatched away and told me to never try to take his phone again. He then got hostile and said if I could not act right, then I could just leave. I asked him what was wrong and he acted as if he were mad at me. I could not understand what I'd done to upset him. I then tried to kiss on him; but he was not too responsive, so I began cleaning his house like I normally did. When I was doing his laundry, a really big bra was in his clothes hamper. I brought it out to show him and he looked surprised. He told me that he was doing his son's family laundry. I also saw a woman's tee shirt and panties in a bag on the door of his spare bedroom. I began thinking to myself, where was the son's laundry? Why was his son's wife bra the only piece of clothing in his possession? One night after service, he was once again in his car. I decided to go to his car and he did not realize that I'd snuck up on him. When I knocked on his car window, he jumped and immediately hung up the phone. He literally yelled at me and told me that I should not have startled him. He told me to back up because people at the church already thought that he showed me favoritism. I became really suspicious. It became clear one Sunday when we were sitting in church and he was smiling at me like he always did; then he kept smiling, but instead of him looking at me, he looked over me so I turned around and noticed this girl smiling back at him. He saw me, so he turned his head. After service, I confronted him about it and he tried to ignore me. I then stood in the sanctuary for a while watching him. The girl did not leave but once she did get up, he was already standing in the back of the church. The girl was talking to someone else and then I saw him sneak in a hug to her. At that point, I knew that my eyes were not playing tricks on me. I was so upset that this man was trying to be a player in the house of God that I left and called him later. Of course, he did not answer. He called me to come over to clean his house on the following Thursday. I went over and this time while cleaning, I saw earrings on his nightstand, a dress and scrubs in his closet. I'd had it at this point, so I called him told him that I saw some earrings on his nightstand and they were not mine. He calmly said okay and that he would call me back because he was at work. While I was awaiting his return call, I got the scissors and tore up the dress and cut holes in the scrubs. I returned them to the closet as if I'd never seen them. I did not want to cry because I wanted to hear what he had to say. He called me back and told me that his son had been at his house and was apparently having an affair. He then got mad and told me that if I did not want to wait for him I was just to leave and leave the key. I asked him why his son would move his family down here if his marriage was on the rocks? He then told me to stop asking questions. When I went to his bathroom, I saw tweezers, glue and facial cleanser in the drawer. I squeezed out the cleanser into the toilet. I tossed out the glue and rubber bands. I took the tweezers, I also saw some hair sheen on his sink and asked him was it his and he said no. I was so mad, I threw the product to the floor and then he picked me up and tried to push me out of his house. I was crying so much, I just knew that he was cheating on me. I was so embarrassed about going to service that night. My eyes were so swollen from the crying. People kept asking me was I okay and I just said yes. When we talked again I told him who I thought it was, he told me that I was crazy and that girl had a boyfriend. He also asked me why I thought he was chasing young booty? I kept telling myself, this dude thinks that I'm crazy. How did he know that she had a boyfriend if he were not talking to her? The following week, I called him so that we could talk. We met at a restaurant and talked. I asked him what happened to us? I asked him if he were gone? I just could not understand. We had just celebrated his birthday a couple of weeks prior and had been going out to eat at our favorite spot every Sunday after service. He told me that he was trying to get himself together and that he was backing away because he still believed I was trying to reconcile with my husband. It was September 2019 when pastor Narc and I began our affair. During this time my husband and I were still married. My husband and I divorce was finalized in July 2020. Then in August 2020, Pastor Narc shared with me that he was trying to get himself together and that he was backing away because he still believed that I was trying to reconcile with my husband, so I asked him how could that be when my ex and I were divorced? Pastor Narc ended up coming to my school and we sat in the parking lot talking and playing for a while. The girl whose number I'd seen the night that I came up to his car was calling him while I was still sitting in his car. He covered up the number, which made it even more suspicious. I was getting ready to cry. I asked him again if it was the same girl and he once again denied it. The following day, I stopped by his house to check on him since he was not feeling well at the restaurant. I went into his room to fold his clothes and then I saw a pair of female pants on the bed, this time I did not say anything. I went into the bathroom and looked in the drawer, saw some rubber bands, cut them up and threw them in the garbage. I then went back in the living room to lay on the couch, then the unthinkable happened, I touched something that appeared to be a caterpillar; but they were really long eyelashes. I held them up to show him and burst out crying. He showed no remorse at all. He didn't say he was sorry. He actually told me that it was my fault that he was doing what he was doing. He said that I tried to hurt him by when I told him that my husband dearly loved me. Therefore, Pastor Narc thought that I was going to leaving him. I thought in my head that he first lied about the main pastor, then about his son and now he blamed me? I stayed with him for a little while longer because I wanted a sensible answer from him. An apology. A hug. I was so confused. I told him that I felt like he was gone and he told me that he was not gone. He told me that he was not seeing anyone and that he was going through something. I stayed as long as I could and then I told him that I was going to his room to lay down. He said I could not and that I needed to go home to get up for work in the morning. He had to go and meet someone from the band so we both left. He talked with me on the phone until I arrived at home. He made sure that I was home before he hung up. I was just too hurt to let this go. I remembered the girl gave me her business card. I used my work number to call her. I first blocked my number and then called her. She actually picked up the phone and what did I hear in the background? Pastor Narc's tv. I disguised my voice and expressed an interest in getting lashes. She told me that she could help me but I would need to call her back from a regular number. I said okay. I then put back on my clothes and went back over to his house. Once I got to the door, I heard that tv. I also heard them having a conversation about Nikes. She was trying to make an excuse for not having them and then he yelled at her, "Nigga, you better get my Nikes" and she just bashfully said okay... okay... and hushed. After that I could hear him walking down the hall. He did not sound sick anymore, which let me know that he was acting again. I began knocking at his front door and then everything got quiet in his apartment. I started saying that I was going to tell his wife, kids and church. I stayed there for about 10 minutes knocking. He was scared to come to the door. I left and returned to my home. I just wanted to see for myself because I knew that I was not crazy. I knew that it was that girl. He called me that night trying to threaten me. He told me that the police were coming to my job to arrest me. He told me that his neighbor saw me at his door. It burned me up because on Thursday night's service, the girl and I were sitting in the same row. I was even conversing with her. He was such a nasty, low down devil. Meanwhile, he was sitting at the organ just acting as if he were God's gift to the world. I could tell that was something he did often. He played it so well. That led me to believe that was common to him. A typical narcissist move. No feeling, no emotion. I can almost hear him say, "Look at this, I have all of my women sitting in here with each other and they do not know that I am playing them all". Just like a demon! Now it makes sense. When he and I were on the phone and he was just speaking openly, he was actually making a list of the women he wanted and the women who he would discard. He actually asked me how many women I thought the main pastor slept with. It was if he were in a competition. How sick and disgraceful.

All the while, I thought that this man was genuine; but he had targeted me and had a plan to manipulate me the entire time. He snatched away my time of grieving in exchange for his own selfish and manipulative ways. How wicked to capitalize upon me instead of consoling me. I trusted this man to share my personal business and my personal space. He was my pastor. He was the one who I should have been able to talk to about my personal problems, but instead he was the devil himself. I later discovered that he was a narcissist.

The Affair – The Discard

From that point on, I knew things were over. This is when the narcissist has secured his new supply. In short, supply is something (I will not even say someone because a narcissist does not care if you are a dog, cat, horse, monkey), the narcissist secures to meet his needs at that time. It fills whatever void he needs fulfilled. I would have rather he told me the truth instead of taking me through all of that. I once again ignored the red flags. I can recall speaking with him on different phone conversations. He would say different things, such as: "I've been acting stand-offish because I'm trying to get myself together (by the way, what 64 year old man says teenage stuff like that?)." He also said, "I'm trying to figure out how I'm going to become your pastor again". Also, I remember after one of our arguments that he staged, he called me a few days later with more of the same and then told me that "two can play at the game". I was so confused. I later realized that he officially made up in his mind that he would see a new girl. A narcissist has to rationalize their behavior. They make up and believe their own lies. If it's real to them, then it should be real for everyone. This is how he made up this entire fiasco of a grand lie, believed the lie and then acted upon the lie. Talk about a psychological game?? This man would drive anyone to drink. He has a head full of loose marbles!! I decided that this was the final straw for me to finally leave that ministry. This man broke my marriage and then he tried to break me. He used me as prey and discarded me! I called the other pastor and informed him why I was leaving. I told him about the affair. I had to have a meeting with him. Little did I know that Pastor Narc invited himself to the meeting. He acted like a fool in the meeting. I could have said a lot of foolish things to him but I knew I was still in the house of God, as well as I was in a meeting with the main pastor at the time. I had just picked up his dry cleaning the day prior. Once I returned home for the night, I pulled the suits out of my closet, got my knife and tore through all of the suits. This was how I was able to express all of the pain that I was feeling. I would never wish this type of pain on anyone. I lost at least 14 pounds during this time. I could not sleep. I had numerous panic and anxiety attacks. I had to constantly pull down strongholds over my mind. I prayed to God that I would not lose my mind or my hair. The main pastor and I talked again and he convinced me to not leave the church. I tried really hard and was able to stay for one month longer. It was the most tormenting month of my life. Just the thought of attending that church was mentally challenging for me. I literally had to quote scriptures just to get through the service. I'd never been in a situation of being cheated on by a pastor and then his new supply and I are all in the same building. When I tell you that I had to pray hard to keep my composure. During that time of torment, pastor Narc and I both had to sit down from our ministerial duties. His reprimand was longer than mine. We could not communicate at all during this time. He was so crazy that at every chance, be it Sunday, Thursday or Saturday morning, he was determined to try and get under my skin. He would stare me down, constantly come near me. Bump into me and try to get me angry. I mean it was the worst and then on top of that, he accused me of keying his car. I had to pull the girl aside to talk with her from a sister in Christ point of view. She did not accept my apology which was to be expected. She would even try to do things make me jealous. Honestly, I wanted to punch him. As a matter of fact, she was the rebound, so she was no one that I needed to concern myself with anyway. Now, did it hurt that now my so called "man" is wrapping his arms around another woman? Yes it did. Did it hurt knowing that I would never lay in his bed while he sang love songs to me again? Yes it did. Did it hurt that he would never feed me again nor have wild and crazy sex? Yes it did. There would be no more long conversations. There would be no more ensuring that he was eating right or him cooking for me. I was literally sick and wanted it to all go away. Little did I know at the time that this was the biggest blessing in disguise.

The Affair-The Trickery

I began asking Holy Spirit about Pastor Narc's behavior. He reminded me how he was when I initially met him. He was not that way. Of course, he may have already been lustful; but he seemed to have changed in many other ways. I even told him that he was acting really different. It's like he was under a spell. Even before we got to this point, sometime during the month of September, I really noticed the change. The demonic spirits were so heavy in that church that if they were to transfer to a person who did not have the Holy Ghost, the spirit could overtake them. This is what I believe happened to him. I mean the devil was making him look like a fool. This man was so gone that he did not care with whom he tried to romance. Visitors, babes in Christ, it simply did not matter. All he wanted were hips, butts, thighs and opportunities. He was on a mission to run through as many women in that church as possible. He was having a field day. I kept asking myself why he would stoop so low to date someone so much younger. He and I were still many, many years apart, but she was even younger! What also got me was the fact that this girl had just started attending the church -she was not a member and not saved. Because he was a manipulator and a user, I knew that he'd targeted that girl. She had just come to a miracle service where the main pastor told her that she would have a business. He asked her if she did hair and she said "yes hair and lashes". As a matter of fact, pastor Narc was in the foyer talking to her that night and I remember waiting to talk to him. He was so slick, I did not know a thing. Honestly, I believed that he must have met her somewhere else and invited her to church. Who knows? I later found out that she was from Kingsland, GA, which is where he went to golf and he may have met her there. I was told that she had a salon in the city in which we both resided, which explains why Pastor Narc was trying to get me out. He probably offered her to stay with him when she came to the city to do hair. He was always trying to work things out to benefit himself. After much prayer, Holy Ghost led me to these videos on YouTube. The videos were on narcissism. All of the videos described Pastor Narc. All of the behaviors. They nailed him to the "T"!! They described a narcissist as someone who you do not want be with. This is where light and darkness could not mix and my spiritual eye had been opened. I had been awakened!!! Narcissists have a lack of empathy and remorse, which is why they can leave you or treat you wrong and not care about it or you. Everything is about them. They are emotionally unstable. Actually, they are sick psychopaths. They are described as demons. The videos also confirmed what I'd been thinking all along. He was playing games the entire time. Our relationship did not mean a thing to him. For eleven months he accused me of cheating on him, when indeed it was him. I tried to think when he would have time to see anyone else. Unless it was on his golfing days, I never suspected him of cheating; but he was quite a flirt. My mom even noticed that. All he said and did was just to lure me in. He targeted me because he thought that I had life insurance money. One of my friends called him "cray-cray" (crazy). Another friend told me that he was just playing games and then the other told me to run because he was the devil. I believe that spirit was sent to take my focus off God. This lasted for a full year. He pawned my possessions, which is why he never gave them back. He did not care about anyone except himself. I honestly do not understand why he believed that he was a pastor...he did not have the characteristics of a pastor. I tried to figure out who ordained him. His characteristics did not develop over night, they must have been his ways for quite some time. They did not just come over night because he was too good at it. I often times wonder, did he really know that he was hurting others? I wonder, how he could wake up every day ready to manipulate others? Had he done it so much that he felt there was nothing wrong about it? Did he even fear God? I honestly believe that he is a reprobate. A reprobate is a wicked person. He is a person foreordained to damnation. As the scripture **Romans 1:28 stated - "And even as they did not like to retain God in their knowledge, God gave them over to a reprobate mind, to do those things which are not convenient."**

The Self Pity

I went through a phase of asking God, why me? In the morning, I would cry. When I woke up out of my sleep, I would cry. When I was at work, I would cry. I was really beating myself up partly because I felt so stupid. I was down in the gutter and on top of that, he went from treasure to trash!!! I felt like I was back in the world again. This is something I did not tolerate while in the world and definitely not now. When I did not know, shame on him; but now that I knew and if I went back, then shame on me! This man had nothing going for himself, which is why I kept asking myself why? Every time I thought about how he caused me to lose my job, I got upset. I felt like I'd just lost myself and lost so much that I had worked hard for before we even met. Then he turned around and treated me so badly. He delighted in hurting me. He was on a mission to make me as miserable as he was. I kept saying to myself, all I tried to do was to help him. I cared about what he ate. Made sure that he was eating healthy. I cared about how they treated him at church, I even used to get into all types of conflict with others at the church because of him. I spent my hard earned money on him. I was there for him when his dad passed. I was there for him and when I look back he wasn't really there for me. It makes me feel so stupid and so used. I was in a vulnerable state. I allowed him to run all over me. You would have thought that he would have shown some type of empathy, but no. The only time that he was nice was when he was getting ready to ask me for something. He knew when my payday was, and he would ask me what's for dinner. He would always say that he felt like a steak. As a man, you would have thought that he would have more tact and not use women; but no, he was so manipulative that he used whomever he could. I had to ask God to forgive me because the thoughts that ran through my head about him were not nice. I wanted him to die an excruciating death and his soul rest in the eternal pit of hell!!! He is so evil. I used to wonder why good people die and bad people stay around forever and it is because God is long suffering. I literally have to pray for him and say that I forgive him because I did not want bitterness to set into my heart. He definitely is not worth me going to prison. It is just sad how people in this world are so cruel and some who are in the pulpit are professing to be pastors. I mean, how can you do that? God is love and how he handled me was everything but love. He does not have a conscious.

Chapter 3

I'm a Survivor–Ran from a Narc

Verbal Abuse–Emotional

When we began, he was really nice; but when he would get upset about something or he felt like I was not listening to him, he would cuss me out. When he got really mad, he would fuss so hard at me and get directly in my face with his spit flying all over. It's like the rage in him was furious. Once he stopped, he would want to have sex and I better not cry. Sometimes when we were having sex, during foreplay, I would sometimes have my back turned and I would be "boo-hoo" crying. Once he turned me over, I would have to quickly wipe my tears and act like I was enjoying the moment. The next thing I knew he would be holding me close, snoring in my ear. He was so insecure at church. Here were a few things that I did that would cause him to verbally abuse me: if he saw me playing on my phone; if I walked out of the sanctuary and was gone for a bit; if he saw me talking with any guy; if I did not have the correct flavor gum for him; at home, if I washed his jeans; if I dried his shirts too long; or if I ordered food from a place that he did not like. Because I was not really getting any attention at home, good or bad to me was better than no attention. I began losing myself. He did not want me to have any friends. He told me to end a friendship that I had for over 15 years. He gave me an ultimatum.

Physical Abuse -

I'm not really sure when this abuse actually began, but he loved to pinch me. He would sometimes try to pin me down. He knew that I was claustrophobic. He was so much bigger than me, hence I gave him the nickname papa bear. I fit perfectly in his arms. He would grab me by the wrist and pull me. Then, as things got worst with us, he tried to choke me. There was a time when his neighbor called the police on us. That night he was trying to choke me and shove me in the bathtub. All I could think about was how a pastor could do that? He swore up and down that I called the police because I closed myself in his wash room and I had my phone. He blamed me for everything. I could try to plead my case until I were blue in the face, but if he felt like he was right in his head, it did not matter what I said. This man knew that his neighbor had just called the animal shelter on him because his dog bit her; yet he still believed her to be a saint. He and his neighbor joined forces to smear my name. This is when his smear campaign began. He had his neighbor call me names and say that she did not like me. Honestly, I never did anything to her. This is how pastor Narc manipulated others into thinking that he was the innocent. Little did they know...

Mental abuse -

This came as a result of him always accusing me of sleeping with the other pastors, the musicians and the other guys at the ministry. He took me golfing once. I thought that he was just trying to spend time with me but no, the good times were short lived because he used the opportunity to scold me for standing up during one of the praise team songs when the bass guitarist was singing. He told me that I was going to learn him one day. He was determined to control me. When I did not listen to him or talk back, the abuse would begin. He told me that I did not need to think for myself and that he would be doing all of the thinking for me. He would tell me that he did not like me but Moses (this is what he named his penis) did. He would always tell me to become subject to him. He told me that my mouth got me in trouble. Thinking back, we also had a lot of non-hostile times. He wanted me to move back to Maryland with him when he was thinking about leaving. He went from one extreme to the other. He would sing to me. He would be spontaneous and cook me breakfast. He loved to feed me. The attention that he gave me was out of this world. He catered to all of me. When we were out, he treated me like a queen. It's like it was just me and him. He made me feel so comfortable being around him that I felt as if I could finally be myself. I mean we would laugh and play around so much. All he did was

FaceTime me. He would FaceTime me while he was on the golf course or In his car. We would sometimes fall asleep together on FaceTime. Alexa was our best friend. We cooked together. We liked a lot of the same foods, so we were even gaining weight together until covid-19, then we began losing weight. Lol. I mean, I really actually thought that we had a pretty good relationship. He told me that he thought that he could never love anyone ever again. In church, he always catered to me. I would be sure to support him while he led his songs. He shared a lot of information with me that he had not shared with others. One of our favorites was watching movies with popcorn, candy and watermelon. Then we would fall asleep on the sofa. I would always fall asleep on top of him. Even though he was fast asleep, he always felt me falling and would pull me up just in time. We really had some great times. I loved our walks with the dog. She was our bodyguard. Lol. I mean we did everything together. We loved to walk by the water. He told me that I had better not go to any of our favorite spots without him. We loved to take pictures and videos. I would trim his brows and ears in my birthday suit. Lol. I would polish his nails with nail hardener. We loved to drink Simply Limeade. He would pour the drink in his mouth and then drain it into my mouth. It would still be ice cold. I could go on and on but I will not. I'm including this for a reason, to show you that we had more good times than bad, which is why the mental abuse was real. It was traumatizing. Imagine someone getting in your head so deep and catering to every part of your body. You're going fall in love, right? Or become deeply infatuated. Then one day–BOOM! Just like that things changed. I was like what happened? I was a wreck when I realized that he was gone (so I thought). I would have panic attacks. I could not sleep. I was crying at my job every day. I lost a lot of weight. I was having anxiety attacks. I was devasted. He was all I knew for the past year. We were together practically every day and when we were not together, we were on the phone or FaceTime. I could not understand how his behavior towards me changed so quickly. I put in so much effort and sacrificed a lot for us. I lost my job, my husband and my luggage because of him. My emotions were everywhere. I would literally have to pray over my mind every night and ask God to keep me alive. I had never been through anything like this before. I can see if we were going break up or something, but we weren't, at least I did not think so. In the beginning I would cry while reminiscing because he would never hold me in his arms again, he would never sing to me again, he would never feed me again, he would never push my hair behind my ear ever again, he would never kiss my girls again and I would never see Moses ever again. I was upset at the fact that someone else would be getting that treatment now. It's like he had my heart in his hand and crushed it to the ground. I was so broken. My heart had a different type of ache. Everything pastor Narc did was spiritually demonic, which means that the impact upon me was magnified by one hundred. He had not only broken into my mind and heart, but also my soul. There was a demonic soul tie that was upon me. It needed to be broken, otherwise because of the depth of the aching, I could have died.

Chapter 4

Shhh....keep this between you and me

I was a secret at the ministry. I would tell him that I did not feel good about being a secret. He told me that he was being careful because he was a private person and that he was trying to protect us. He said because he was a pastor that it would not appear seemly because he and I still had spouses. Even though we both knew that he was not with his wife and my husband and I were separated at the time. When we saw each other in church, we would casually talk. He would show me enough attention so I would not question what he was doing. Looking back, he was so good at this, no one would suspect if he were playing games with other women or not. I told him that I wanted to go out, like to the movies, out of town, overall just go out on dates, and so we did. We would go out of town, we would meet at the park and walk or look at the water, eat, talk., and take pictures. Lol. We both loved taking pictures. He appeared to have really been into me. It was like we were a real couple. He was doing everything that I needed him to do. He was being the man that I needed him to be. At church, he would always look out for me. He would tell me to go and get a seat at our favorite restaurant after Sunday service. He would stay behind at church and by the time he arrived at the restaurant, I would have already ordered his food. During those times, I was really happy. I really did feel like I was in a real relationship. Sometimes after church, we would just go to his house and order in our Sunday meal. Whatever we did, we were always together. He told me that his son and his son's family were moving down and that they were going to be staying at his house for a few weeks. I asked him if he was going to introduce me to them and to my surprise, he did. We actually communicated on a few instances. They were really nice.

Chapter 5

True Deliverance– True Repentance

I was becoming truthful with God and really feeling sorry about my behavior. Over time, things began to get kind of redundant and we just argued all of the time and then would make-up. He had pushed me to the point where I just did not care what I would say to him anymore. Then he would act as if I was saying rude things just to have said them. Whenever I mentioned what he had done, he would never take ownership of it. I knew what I was doing was wrong and he had not said anything about divorcing his wife. I knew that I did not want to remain in this rut forever and I shared this with him. He would always put the focus back on my ex-husband and me. He would never come clean about his plans, all he said was that he wanted to move to the next level with me. I honestly did not know what that meant and he never took the time to explain it to me either. Because there were no concrete answers, and by this time he began going back and forth, I began seeking God. I knew that I could not say that pastor Narc was my husband because he was still married. By this time, my divorce had been finalized. I finally put my foot down and seriously asked God to intervene. I asked God to trouble the water because I could not get out of this rut alone. God did just that.

What I learned was that when you ask God for something, you need to be ready, because you do not know what that trouble will look like. Boy did I hit a doozy this time. Going through this caused the worst pain I'd ever felt in my entire life. I literally had to pray over my mind every day and ask God to keep me alive. I was having panic and anxiety attacks. I was not sleeping or eating. I was depressed and crying all of the time, even while at work. I would not have wished this pain on my worst enemy!

With all the evil thoughts that I had about him. I literally had to tell someone to keep me from actually going through with them. Just writing this is painful. Once we were reprimanded by the main pastor, we could not communicate for thirty days. After which time, I called him to tell him that I forgave him for all of the lies and manipulation, etc. The nerve of him — he kept telling me that I did not see myself in any of it. He was so arrogant and prideful that he would not take full responsibility for playing games with me yet he was the one who started all of that. I told him that he had no intention of leaving me, but he was trying to cheat and shift

Lightness and Darkness Cannot Mix

me around. I did not realize that he was not committed to me the entire time. I only found out about this one because the new supply came over to his apartment. Because she was extremely insecure, she tried to make herself known. In the beginning, I was really upset, but now that I look back on things, I am truly grateful for her. She is the reason I was able to leave. If there were other girls, they kept themselves a secret. I had to go through the process of first forgiving myself and then I asked God to forgive me. I then repented. I remember a few counselors told me to watch out because Pasto Narc will try to come around again. He was not finished with me. A part of me wanted to smile because I still had deep feelings for him. I was longing for him every day. I missed our conversations, whether we were laughing or discussing something. A piece of my heart had been removed. I believe I felt this way because he knew exactly what I needed and hit it on the head. It was like something I had always wanted came true and then it was suddenly taken away. Can you imagine how much that hurts? I am literally getting teary eyed as I write. I want to include the details in case you can relate. If you are going through similar circumstances, I want you to really understand that I understand. Pastor Narc and I talked on the phone and saw each other a few more times. Each time he was all over me. He told me how much me missed me. He chain-dialed my phone. Christmas week and then on Christmas day, he called and Face Timed me so many times, it was unreal! I decided to pay him a visit because he was acting really crazy. When I went to his house, he was terrible. This man was truly sick. All he thought about was sex. It was an addiction for him.

His house was so dirty. It looked as if it hadn't been cleaned since I cleaned it last. I asked him where his girls were – did they leave him alone for the day? He asked me to stop. I told him that I missed our old relationship and that it will never be the same again. Later, he came over to my mom's house and hugged her for one last time as well. He acted like we were good again; but in the back of my head, I knew that I were done. I was able to see him one last time and then I decided I had enough. I blocked him in my phone. I truly wanted to repent and turn away from this sin. I noticed that it was not even good to talk to him, let alone see him. (I am having anxiety attacks just talking about this.) I told my mom that if he tried to reach out to her or stop by her house, not to allow him. I told her that I was really serious about having no contact with him. The days are now getting better and I am growing stronger. In the past, I would have had another man to mask the pain; but I decided to do it God's way. I wanted to allow Him to heal my wounds and make me whole again before I got into another relationship. This is not easy, but I trust God. Day by day I am meditating and staying in God's Word to free my mind from this darkness.

Chapter 6

Which would you choose, Hell on earth for a season or Hell with the devil for an eternity?

I was thanking God every day that I did not die in my sins. I had enough hell on earth with that man, there was no way I would remain with pastor Narc and bust hell wide open! I would not allow anyone or anything to make hell my final resting place. The devil is a liar. When pastor Narc and I did talk, I told him that he was going to burst hell wide open and he replied that I was going with him. I told him that I was not because I'd truly repented. He did not take his reprimand seriously. He was still playing games with other females. He was more concerned about a nice looking suit and his gift of song. His soul was the last thing on his mind. You would think that he would be fearful for his soul.

Now, I only want to surround myself with positive people. I am walking my deliverance. This will not happen overnight. When dealing with a narcissist, there are layers of the demonic that have to be addressed. You have to get to a point of being refined and coming out as pure gold. Fasting (a must) and prayer (decreeing and declaring) will get you there. Also, you have to admit what you did wrong and embrace what God is trying to do through you. This state is a critical stage because you can either allow what happened to you heal you or break you. You must make a conscious effort to speak who God says you are over your life every day.

Chapter 7

Do you Fear the Lord?

*H*e really did not fear the Lord. One day, I told him that I was totally wrong. I said that he reminded me of my dad. I told him that I was wrong because my dad was an upright man. This pastor really stirred things up for me. There was always conflict with him. It's like he loved chaotic situations. He cussed like a sailor. He would do evil things intentionally just because he could. He was a liar. He was extremely childish. He was embarrassing to be around in the public. I remember we were leaving a hotel and he wanted some lotion. There was a housekeeping cart in the hall and he just helped himself to her supplies thinking that the containers were lotion. Once he noticed that there were shampoo and conditioner instead of lotion, he tossed them in the garbage. I asked him to return the containers to the cart. He told me he would not. He had no regard for others whatsoever. Actually, he was only concerned about himself.

Chapter 8

Have you been turned over to reprobate?

I began a thorough study about narcissism and can truly say that this man was a narcissist! If you look at the characteristics of a narcissist, it replicates that of the devil. As I began studying narcissism, I discovered that they never change. It is unwise to spend energy trying to change them. Because they lack empathy, they do not feel the pain they inflict upon others. Thinking back to my situation, it was dangerous being with Pastor Narc because I never knew when he was going to flip the script on me. Narcissists come into your life to kill, steal and destroy. They kill your dreams and spirit, steal your joy and destroy your sanity. I mean he left me for dead. He saw into my psyche and met my emotional needs. His motives were to get me to a place where

I would first trust him and then he could control me. This lasted for a while until I caught onto him. This man hurt me so deeply. He treated me terribly in the end. All I ever tried to do was be there for him in several ways, only to be rebuffed. This man never apologized to me. Instead, he flipped the script. He has been playing women for such a long time. I remember he made a remark about his wife. He asked me had I ever seen a 70 year old body and then he smirked and laughed. I felt so bad for his wife. I believed that lady really loved him and he manipulated her as well. Pastor Narc shared with me early on in our relationship that his wife was a breast cancer survivor. I honestly believe that her breast cancer was a result of the stress that she endured from his constant infidelity. You would think that he would be there for her now; but rather he is with other women. You wonder why people like this take a long time to leave this earth. I honestly believe that he has been turned over to reprobate. He is so far gone that he does not know right from wrong. I believe that he is not even happy with himself. A narcissist will remain immature and selfish no matter the age. At some point God will lift His hand. I know that God is sovereign and long-suffering; but I'm really wondering if God has lifted His hand from this man already. When I say that he is terribly evil, I mean just that. He has been doing it for so long, he doesn't even care. He has a form of godliness but denies His power. He is backslidden. No one is immune. I stated earlier that the demonic spirits that make up the narcissist are Jezebel, Ahab & Leviathan. Pastor Narc exemplified the characteristics of each.

Ahab –

During my studies, I learned that Ahab was the most evil ruler that ever existed. He and his evil wife Jezebel, were a toxic tag team. She convinced Ahab to build an altar in Samaria, which was to be dedicated to the false god, Baal. Ahab had to have his way and when he did not, he threw temper tantrums. There was an instance where he wanted Naboth's land, however; Naboth refused the offer. Did you know that Jezebel had Naboth killed because Ahab threw a fit? Read it for yourself in ***1 Kings 21:7-10, 15***. I believe Ahab definitely had narcissistic ways but my question is, was he completely narcissistic? Because at some point, he repented of his wickedness. Below are a few characteristic in which I saw the Pastor Narc identify with the Ahab spirit.

1. He was not a strong spiritual leader. He caused conflict and confusion with every situation he encountered with the people and leadership.

2. He had very low self-esteem. If I did not compliment him on the song that he led in church that day or if I did not compliment him on the suit that he was wearing, he would bring it up in my face and make statements such as: "How come everybody else complimented me on my singing and/or suit and I didn't?"

3. He would come off as being a very nice person but behind closed doors the real demonic Pastor Narc will come out.

4. He feared abandonment and was extremely clingy, needy and helpless. This is the reason why he would always accuse me of wanting to leave him. He would call me all the time. I had to be under him often and he had to always know where I was and what I was doing all of the time. He always feared that I was going to leave him for and return to my husband.

5. He was afraid of rejection. Once again, he always thought that I was cheating on him.

6. He carried unforgiveness. I believe there was a traumatic event in his childhood or life as an adult that caused him to become a narcissist. Instead of forgiving the person(s), his pride and ego allowed him to harbor unforgiveness.

Leviathan –

1. He was extremely prideful – he did not have a pot to piss in but thought that he was better, looked better and preached better than anyone else. Although he had ugly feet, bad credit and no money, in his head, he was a ladies man!!!

2. His mind twisted reality – I often times labeled him as delusional even before I knew with whom I was dealing. When we talked, he would create these off-the-wall stories. He would keep asking the same questions over and over as if he wanted to catch me in a lie. Then once I told him the truth, he would pause and tell me he did not believe me.

3. He was sickly but was too arrogant to really seek healing and deliverance–He had headaches because of those boils all over his head and body. He would always get sick when one was surfacing. I really do believe that he was stricken with them because of his consistent sinful lifestyle.

4. He also has a few other serious afflictions in his body, such as high blood pressure, gout and diabetes.

Jezebel –

1. Controlling – He was obsessed with ensuring that I did not communicate with my friends. He made sure that I was always at his apartment. He insisted on dressing me; and if it were a piece of clothing or even shoes that he did not like, he would be sure to tell me. He made me put a chemical in my hair after I'd gone completely natural. There is so much more that he tried to control that I would be writing for days if I continued.

2. Manipulative – This actually began from the start. It started when he smiled and spoke to me on numerous occasions during the "Holy Convocation 2019". It did not matter the situation, he manipulated me.

3. Jealous – He was jealous of me because I had a lot going for me in my life. It were as if, he wanted to be me. He was living his best life through me at my expense!

4. Demanding – Here is the crazy part. We were both a part of a wealth building group in which I'd invested some money. Well, of course, I had to make an investment for him because he was broke. In this group, each person who invested money had a chance to receive a donation. He noticed that everyone in my group was getting paid except for him. I shared with him that he would need to begin working before he could get paid. According to him, because he feels privileged, pastor Narc decided to make a complaint against me. Wow…go figure. He was demanding to get paid. Remember, I was the person who made his contribution, so if anything, I should have received his payout. He really felt that he could go over my head and get paid when he did not contribute. The nerve of that idiot! Long story short, I'd already spoken with the supervisor and explained everything to her. She thankfully sided with me. He never got paid. He was fuming.

5. Sexually impure and selfish – Yes, after I came to the knowledge that he had multiple partners, I actually felt really dirty. I immediately made an appointment with my doctor to ensure that I did not have any diseases. Thankfully, I was clean. While he sat at his desk at work, he would be on the phone masturbating while talking to me. Also, when he told me he was in meetings, he would really be at some woman's house. Oh, God, I am so grateful that You were covering me. This animal, I believe could have sex all day if he had it his way. Can you imagine someone having sex multiple times in a day and with different partners? I remember, he would always have me to wash his male body parts. I guess at least he did have enough sense to wipe off before moving on to the next victim for the day. Of course, he did not care about his health; but he did not care about my health either. If he did, he would not have put me in that predicament.

6. Lies – This became progressively worse. He lied about everything. You know how someone can lie so much that they begin to believe their own so called truths. He was so good at lying that he could lie to my face with a straight face and sound really convincing.

7. Desire for power and leadership- He would always tell me that the main pastor could not teach and that he always taught the same message every week.

Pastor Narc also used to tell people that he was the main pastor at the church. He told me that it was going to be his church one day.

8. Cannot stand to be told no – I remember once I told him that I was not going to give him any money. He constantly annoyed me about it until I had to lie. He became angry. Each day, somehow, he would bring up the same question about the money in our conversation thinking that my answer would change. After all of the pressure, I finally gave in and sent him the money.

9. Insecure – he was always seeking approval from me and others. Whenever he ministered at church, if I spoke highly of another person, he would get quiet and then later, he would ask why I did not compliment him? Or he would tell me that everyone else complimented him on his attire and why didn't I? He would look himself in the mirror and would say something negative about a body part in hopes of me saying something nice. This was his way of truly showing insecurity and seeking affirmation without actually admitting it.

10. Loves to provoke people until they get angry and the blames them – I could be in a really good mood and then pastor Narc would just find something about which to complain. It would take me a while to respond; and when I did, it would just dig a hole

Lightness and Darkness Cannot Mix

to the point of me becoming angry. By this time, I would begin yelling back and behaving just as ridiculous as him. Once I was at my peak of anger, he would ask me in a calm way, what was wrong or why was I so mad? He blamed my anger on me.

11. Enjoys starting arguments – It became a part of our relationship to argue. We argued about the least to the greatest of situations. Upon noticing this, I would just ignore him or walk away from the heat.

12. Constant chatter in the mind – He was always plotting and thinking of how he could manipulate someone. He would also come up with some of the most bizarre thoughts and stories. He would literally make up stories and believe them. His lies were his truth.

13. Wants to shut down the Holy Spirit – He tried his hardest to stop me from praying outside of church. He also operated in religion. He did not operate in Holy Spirit. His tongue was full of profanity and lies. The Holy Spirit cannot dwell in an unclean house.

14. Dominant–He would use his voice to dominate the conversation by talking over me. He would try to dominate the TV and whatever we were to watch.

15. Intimidates–Because of his height and weight, he felt as if he could intimidate others.

Chapter 9

Just when you thought everything was alright, you allowed the devil to step back in

I was doing well in ministry and my relationship with God and then I got caught up. After I found out who this man was, I really felt stupid. I felt used and abused. I felt like I was in a nightmare from which I could not wake up. Such evil thoughts were rolling around in my head. I wanted him to die a gruesome death!! I wanted him to pay for every dollar that I spent on him. I wanted him to pay for every lie that he told me. I wanted him to pay for playing me right to my face. What kind of sick and heartless person does those things? HIM. He was sick!!! Then on top of that, he tried to deny ever knowing me. He cared more about being out on the streets than me. I had gotten into so much conflict with people at that cult and then he used everything that I ever told him against me. That man was truly sick. I thought that I was in a place with God where I would not fall in that area. The crazy thing about this is that I was not even looking for this. I do not attend church to have affairs with pastors. Week by week, I watched this man playing with God. In that case, I was too. Although I never gave up my prayer life, I was just as wrong as he was. The difference between us was that I had a conscious and he did not. He obviously did not care about my body or even my health. He was sleeping with me and other women all at the same time. I let my guard down and gave the devil a front row seat into my life — VIP style.

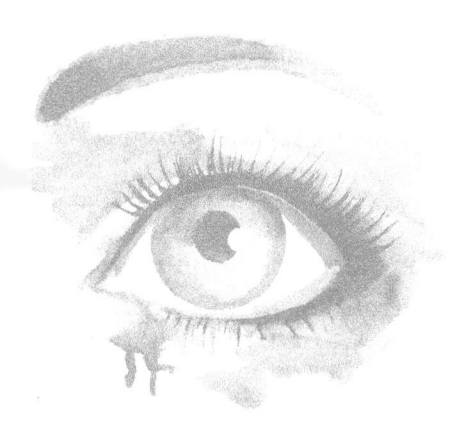

Chapter 10

Get thee behind me Satan!

*E*ven after the affair ended, we saw each other a few times. We talked and Face Timed a few more times as well. Each time we talked or saw each other, he was getting worse and worse. I did not even want him to touch me. I remember he was in his office masturbating. He did not care that other church people were around. All he thought about was sex. He was addicted. I was church raped. I was stripped of my dignity, joy, peace, happiness and trust. All I wanted to do was to serve the man of God. I was in a rut and I could not get out. Still, in my mind, I would miss the friendship that we had and then I had to remind myself it was not real. I fell for a fantasy. I sought counseling to actually talk this out. I'd already worn out my friends ears from talking about it so much. I realized that no one would be able to deliver me from this. I had to do something on my part. I had to say, "Get thee behind me Satan!" Now that he is gone, I can now grieve my dad. This man never cared to even realize the pain that he caused me. I still had to forgive him. The Bible speaks of in Matthew 5:44, "But I say unto you, love your enemies, bless them that curse you, do good to them that hate you, and pray for them that despitefully use you, and persecute you. I can truly say that God was with me the entire time. Matthew 28:20 states, "Teaching them to observe all things whatsoever I have commanded you. And lo, I am with you always, even unto the end of the world." Amen. I know that we often look at the bad in a situation; but God wants to know what we have learned. How can our testimony help to bring someone else through? I am here to say that I am running for my life. I will not look back like Lot's wife. The price of the consequence is too great. My soul being at peace means more to me than a bit of pleasure on earth. Another thing, that man never cared for me or himself because if he did, he would not have put either of us in jeopardy of our final resting place being in the pit of hell.

How did I Come to meet the Narcissists, anyway? Since when did ministry become about us and no longer about God?

Ungodly Connections – I was scrolling through my Facebook page one day and one of my Facebook friends shared with me a pastor preaching online. I was curious about what he was discussing, so I stopped to view the video. Lo and behold, the man was a good teacher. So from that point, I'd been following that pastor. Little did I know at the time, my life would forever be changed. This was the beginning of my experience with witchcraft. At this cult, the pastor who I began following through Facebook, was the main pastor, the overseer and Pastor Narc, was the pastor under the main pastor. The main pastor had several pastors under him. The more I studied about witchcraft, the more I was able to identify with what was going on at the cult that I attended. I was also beginning to understand the occult leader's focus, which was on the membership, co-dependency, sex, wealth, and healing/miracles/signs/wonders. As sad as it may sound, Christians are some of the most vulnerable and gullible groups of people. We are more prone to being deceived than any other religious groups known. I believe that this warlock had been initiated into the occult. So, I began conducting research about how witchcraft actually works. From what I've been hearing from ex-occult leaders, there are a plethora of demonic avenues to obtain such powers.

- Many of us seek to attend a church service as a part of doing the right thing. We are trying to change our lives for the better. We want to have a higher deity to call upon. Prophets and pastors who are riding dirty have grown to know this! These are the types of round table conversations in which they engage. I asked God why this happened to me. He led me to a resource that explained the bottom line and painted a clearer picture of what had happened. I'd heard before of churches practicing witchcraft; but I never paid attention because I never really knew what it was. This is what I see today. The word of God simply states – **Hosea 4:6 – "My people are destroyed for lack of knowledge: because thou hast rejected knowledge, I will also reject thee, that thou shalt be no priest to me: seeing thou hast forgotten the law of thy God, I will also forget thy children."** In its simplest term, witchcraft is demonic control. It is someone having power over another, controlling another. **www.briticannica.com says that it is the exercise or invocation of alleged supernatural powers to control people or events, typically involving sorcery or magic.** I really do believe that this warlock was using witchcraft to gain viewership to his Facebook page as well as use the witchcraft to control innocent people's minds. I say that because after I listened to his message on FB, I listened to it several times thereafter. I even shared the FB message with my other FB friends. There was an International pastor who was sharing his experience of being a warlock; and he came out with the truth of that dark world after no longer wanting to engage in those fraudulent and demonic practices. A portion of what he shared was describing the method types and methods of control funneled through witchcraft. That pastor wanted power, money, big membership. There is a witchcraft ritual for practically anything and anyone you want to control. Anyway, my formal warlock cult leader had a lot of International pastor friends and he visited their country a lot. That country was known for practicing witchcraft.

I believe that he was going over to that country to gain demonic powers. As I was reading through the measures that one takes to obtain power, I was simply blown away at the desperation of the pastors. These pastors had become a part of a secret society. They visited witches. As the now transformed pastor explained, he had to make a sacrifice to three different altars (idols). His first sacrifice was for the devil. If he gave the devil what he wanted then the devil would give him what he wanted. The second sacrifice caused him to operate under strange fire. This type of sacrifice brought upon the presence of evil forces. Then his final sacrifice was to call upon the water spirits. Upon completing that ritual, he belonged to the marine spirit. Here is where the deception came into play. After receiving these powers, one would receive cover and protection so that no one would suspect him from operating with strange powers. The people would think that he was operating under the powers of the Holy Ghost. The initiation into this occult was an extensive process. I felt like I were reading a book about wizardry. I was really in awe after hearing the measures people take out of desperation and addiction. You would even be given a name once you became a part of the secret society. I remember the people would call my former occult leader, "major." They would yell out, "prophecy, major." I used to wonder why they would say that. Some other names that the occult leader would use a lot were sons. We were his sons.

Spiritual mothers and fathers. This is common terminology used referencing being a part of an occult. These are the powers that I believe he wanted based upon the extremity of what was going on at that cult I attended.

- Membership – My former occult leader would always brag about how many social media followers he had. If membership decreased, there would be competitions for us, the members, to help bring in more members. He would award the person who brought in the most members with cash. Then there was the witchcraft. Instead of the occult leader trusting God for the membership to grow, he wanted a faster way. In his meetings and weekly services, that the building had to be packed. There was also witchcraft influences that could be done to pack the buildings. Here, multi (a charm), was a point of contact, that was used for drawing in people or things. The multi would be placed in the location of where a crowd was wanted and the charm would be prepared by the occult leader before the service or the meeting. There was a way that this occult leader could obtain power over us by making a sacrifice and preparing charms and spells. When people came under this occult leader, they were immediately possessed and controlled by the occult leader. This was the reason we were called sons and daughters. The more I educated myself,

Lightness and Darkness Cannot Mix

the more sense it made to me. One of the associate pastors at the cult I attended would always refer to us as "daughter". He would greet me as daughter and not by my name. We were being controlled by a spell. This is what makes this once upon a time church, now a cult!

- Co-Dependency – Needing validity. Needing to belong. Needing to feel loved. He wanted people there who would do and not talk back. Do not question his decision making. When I left the occult, the occult leader had a conversation with me. One thing he told me was that he would not give me his blessing for leaving and that I had the potential to be great. In my research, I began to understand why the occult leader made that remark to me. According to research, one can obtain demonic powers by visiting international pastors and prophets who were already operating in witchcraft. In my case, since he was practicing witchcraft, he was telling me that by remaining under him and performing certain rituals, the anointing on my life would be magnified. I would be a more powerful prayer warrior and minister. As for him, I believe that during his international visits, he was traveling to the places where his most powerful prophet friends obtained their powers.

- Sex – This was a quick and easy avenue to transfer demonic spirits. Those demonic soul ties were the worst. This allows for spells to continue controlling people. This occult leader slept with many of the women and men there. He even had married men and women sleeping with him. Several of us who were married resulted in divorce. We were being pulled to him through satanic powers and neglected our spouses. His goal was to have us all to himself. This is what happened to me. Because of the anointing that was so heavy in my life, for the first four years, those spells were not able to work on me. Then due to my vulnerabilities, with my dad passing and feeling alone in my marriage, the demonic door was opened to having the spell cast upon me.

- Wealth – There were incantations and chanting while praying occult prayers. He would always get our ear and then manipulate with the offering. There was always a reason to collect the offerings. He would always say things like, "There are about ten of you that God has put on your heart to give $50," and because of what he'd spoken, everyone wanted to be in that number because they believed they would receive something special from God. What would happen was, many more people including the 10 would be in the line to give. Those were just mind game fraudulent tricks. Those tricks made him wealthy.

- Healing/Miracles/Signs/Wonders – This occult leader used to disseminate oil to some of us and he also prepared a special oil that only he could use when laying hands on people. There was even an ID number and car VIN forensic prophecy. There were also divination boards which explained the accurate prophecies of current events, as well as personal information about one's life.

Chapter 11

The Importance of having a father in your life-

*I*t is important to have a father in your life. I was not taught what type of man to avoid or allow in my space. I remember that I always enjoyed hanging around older people. I also enjoyed being around older men. I must have always been longing for my dad. I hated that we never had a chance to bond. I wonder what life would have been like if I had grown up with my dad in my life. I've made so many mistakes in life because he wasn't around. I cannot re-live my childhood to try and get it right; but going forward, I can trust my Heavenly Father to Father me. He will show me the way. He will protect me from the wolves. He will give me His wisdom so I can become a woman who attracts the right man.

Chapter 12

You don't know the cost of my oil -

I soon realized that what happened to me does not happen to everyone. I know that I have been chosen as a mouthpiece for God at this time. Trying to explain what happened to me to others has been a challenge. Many did not and still do not understand. It takes you experiencing an awakening. It takes your spiritual eye being opened and seeing through that eye instead of a natural eye. When I say that I had almost lost myself completely, I mean just that! I could have died in my sins. What seemed to have been a blessing or favor ended up being a trick of the enemy. Satan is consistently seeking whom he may devour. Satan was after my mind. Satan was after my ministry. Satan was after my anointing. Satan knew that I was a terror in the body of Christ. Satan had wind of the impact that I would have in winning souls to Christ Jesus, so he tried to shut me down! There was a great stronghold over my mind. All of this was wearing me down: the pain; the humiliation; the rejection; the abuse; the backbiting; the manipulation; and the trauma. In the beginning, I was scared to fall asleep because my mind and my heart were both hurting so bad. I just could not believe how I had ever gotten into something like this. Then with the ministry being involved, I was even more devastated. I'd been in ministry all of my life and never experienced anything like this. I kept asking myself, how can people be so evil? How can people carry out the same behaviors that are outside of the ministry and bring them into the ministry? Then on top of that, walk around as if they are not hurting others? While this man was numb to hurting people, I had to forgive him. I had to no longer focus on what he did to me but focus on becoming whole. As I am still working through that process, I am free to talk to God. I talk to my accountability partners, cry, worship God, scream, and speak out affirmations of who God says I am. Although this healing process is not easy, I have to make a conscious decision that today I win. Today, I am an overcomer. Today, strongholds are being torn down. Today, the demonic soul ties are broken. I am intentionally walking in the spirit–DAILY. I give no place to the devil. When the lingering thoughts from my past try to surface, I cast down the imagination. I remind myself that I have forgiven the predator and all who hid behind the rock but did not throw it. This has been rough because I've never been able to do it before. I chose to not get into another relationship to mask the pain. I trust God. I trust that He will deliver me. He will make me the woman of God that He has called me to be. At this point in my life, I am not even ready for another man or relationship. I am daily giving God my pain. The anointing on my life is so heavy. The price of this oil was great. It nearly cost my life, but God knew all along what He was doing. He just needed to get me to a rock bottom place in order to build me back up again in Him. Preaching could not deliver me from this trial. This trial was one where I had no other choice but to strengthen my relationship with the Almighty King of Kings.

This pain was so deep, I felt like I could not get out of the pit. It was like a nightmare from which I could not awaken. The torment was unbearable. I would oftentimes say, "God, where are you?"

I thought that if anybody had my back it was pastor Narc. I thought that if there was anyone who I could trust it was pastor Narc. He ended up being one of my worst enemies. The pain and betrayal from that was unbearable. He knew how I was being treated there and he always told me that he was trying to shield me. When this happened I felt naked. God was showing me to not rely upon man but to lean on and trust Him. Being isolated did not feel good at all; but for what I was walking in, it was definitely necessary. I believe that I talked so much to my friends about this that they would sometimes not answer their phone, or they would quickly end our conversation. This is how God wants it. He wants a chance to show me that He is God. He is the one who changes our current and future situations. He just wants us to step out in faith and believe Him. He wants us to lean on Him. He wants our problems and shortcomings. He longs for our life so that we can be better equipped disciples for Him. His kingdom will expand and it takes wounded warriors like me to allow His will to be manifest on the earth. Many people want this oil; but they cannot bear it's cost. Believe me, if I could have changed anything about this and still be anointed, I would have changed meeting pastor Narc. It was not only necessary for me, but for many of you who are reading about what I went through. Do not ever think that you have to go through this alone. God loves and cares about you so much. He would go to great lengths to ensure that you are complete in Him.

This real life situation that I suffered for five years was the most life changing event ever. Lightness and darkness cannot mix. You cannot serve two masters. You are either going to choose to be in the Kingdom of God or in the kingdom of darkness. In the Kingdom of God, you go through professing that Jesus is Lord and then you are saved and adopted into the family. Then you receive the gift of the Holy Ghost to help you navigate your life. However, in the kingdom of darkness, you will go through the process of re-birth through a spiritual initiation. Your temple becomes the temple of the newly-born demon. There was a lot of darkness in that pastor. Was he always that way? I do not think so. How did this happen? People are not born a narcissist, they develop into narcissism. This disorder is developed during childhood or a traumatic event. Somewhere down the line, he suffered some type of neglect and lack of love from a parent or he was always having to earn his parent's love. I remember he shared with me that he was his mother's favorite and that he missed her so much. His dad was not in his life. His would always tell me that he is his father's son. For some reason, he held resentment and unforgiveness in his heart either towards his mom or dad. Instead of seeking clinical help, he formed a false self. Because he was in such pain, in any relationship, he would initially come across as a nice person; but is true nature would shortly emerge. We were good when I catered to his every need but the moment I stopped giving to him, he began acting out. I remember I would call him my twin. A narcissist will become a chameleon. The narcissist will become whomever you need him to be. His life is empty so he takes on your life. Although the person who he is manipulating is vulnerable, the narcissist sees that person as a good source of supply; whether that person can supply him financially, emotionally, or physically, etc. The narcissist becomes bored easily, especially if you are losing value to him. I was trying my hardest to make him happy. My life was great. I had a career. I had plans of starting a business. All the while, I thought that he was supporting me and backing me. The whole time, he was jealous and envious of me because he experienced so many failures in his life. His goal was to tear my life apart. Misery loves company. Sadly, after he realized that I was not falling for his game anymore, he continued to smear my name. From what I was told, the entire church knew about us. People from the church would call to check on me. I could determine from their tone that they had been engaging in conversations about the situation. Different members were trying to get me to return to that cult. Lastly, the unthinkable happened. He had flying monkeys. Flying monkeys are little puppets who are controlled by the Narcissist. In their eyes the narcissist is the victim and he cannot do any wrong. His main flying monkey was his new supply at the time. Another one of his flying monkeys was a little girl whom he hated. How did I know this? He talked badly about her all of the time behind her back. He was also using her for her money as well. When he and I were together, she would call him so much. He would literally see her calling and purposefully not pick up the phone. I'd always wondered, as much as she called him, was he having sex with her as well? He had previously shared with me that she slept with everyone, which is how I knew her business. There was also another guy at the church who had shared similar news with me about her behavior as well. Pastor Narc gave his flying monkeys my home address. One Sunday evening, the new supply at the time kept calling my phone and messaging me. She harassed me all that afternoon and evening. She was really adamant about talking to me. While having these back to back phone calls with her, my doorbell rang. I opened it and saw one of the flying monkeys standing at my door. Mind you, this little girl was pregnant. I asked her why was she at my house and she said that she googled me. She came there with the intent to bring harm to me. I told her to leave and that I was going to call the police. Thereafter, I picked up the phone and the other flying monkey was on the line. I asked her if that was what they were doing, and she claimed to not know. I told her that my ex-husband was going to be mad and she had the nerve to tell me that she did not care what my ex-husband thought. Mind you, just so that she would not be in my business, I referenced my ex as my husband. Then she had the nerve to say oh, I knew you were with your husband. She behaved crazier and crazier. Now she thought she knew me? Of course, I assume she did know a few things about me due to pastor Narc. I guess they thought they were scaring me when they came over. In a way I really wanted to retaliate; but I had to remember that I had a career and I have a really good life. I had a lot to lose; on the other hand, neither of them did not. They both lived in an apartment. Drove cheap cars. One was pregnant with no goals and the other was in a failing business and living with a married pastor. So, upon looking at my life and the cost of losing my lifestyle then looking at their life, there was no comparison. I decided that I would bite that bullet and choose my battles wisely. It made me cringe for a while because I know that they felt as if I were afraid and they had the upper hand; but I had to put aside my pride and allow the authorities to handle things. Later on that evening shortly after dark, I heard a bump outside. When I went outside of my door, there were raw eggs thrown all over my front porch, drive way, garage door and my ex-husband's truck. I called the police and reported the incident. He helped me clean the egg off of my ex-husband's truck and waited until I finished cleaning the rest of the egg off my property. He said that they would not return but if they did, I should try to get a picture of the vehicle and then call them back. They returned after they saw me enter my house. I once again called the police and as I was talking, one of the police officers asked me if they were really church folk and I said unfortunately yes. He then said that those girls had serious issues and I totally agreed.

Even someone outside of the church noticed the demonic in operation by their actions. This narcissistic pastor led those girls to behave that way. There was nothing Godly or holy about how they treated me and my property. These were people who I saw in the church every Sunday and Thursday. This is the type of fruit that was being produced from under the leadership of the cult. Granted, it is sad that those girls have no clue as to how they were being used. They did not realize that they would be cheated on, discarded and smeared one day. As a result of the flying monkeys egging my ex-husband's vehicle and my home, I was advised to file an injunction against them. The craziest thing about it was that they filed one against me. Of course, that was most likely pastor Narc's idea. He must have forgotten that I had evidence. His new supply at the time was such a liar. She lied to the police about her name. Actually, she had so many aliases, she could have very well forgotten her name. Anyway, when I was served papers from them, the reason for their injunction was hilarious. I guess they just needed to make something up to try and prove their reason for egging my home and vehicle. Just from the new supply paperwork, I noticed that he'd provided her my work address There were discrepancies in the paperwork, which was to be expected because pastor Narc had a bad memory. It would have made more sense to not file the injunction against me, especially if he did not have all correct information; but knowing pastor Narc, he was always right! He was really making the flying monkeys look even more like stupid puppets. Pastor Narc never showed up at the hearing because I noticed his name listed in the waiting room. Due to covid, the hearing was virtual. He clearly gave himself away about being with the new supply. I guess after he realized that I could see his name, he left the waiting room. The narcissist is really not intelligent to say the least. Unfortunately, our hearing was postponed to a later date. By the time you are reading this, my hearing will have transpired. With the narcissist, the process is always the same. It does not matter who you are. I opened my life up to you, the reader, to show you that deception can be directly in front of you and you not even know it. As a Christian, we must strengthen our relationship with God. We are living in perilous times. There are many backslidden pastors, prophets, teachers, you name it who are out to destroy your relationship with God. As you read through my real life story, you see where even I was living blindly. I was in a relationship with a married pastor. This was a double no-no. If you understand the spirit world, there were strong demonic forces in operation.

The witchcraft that was in operation at this cult channeled through the main occult leader led me into this darkness. I can recall after I'd left the ministry a lady who had also left that ministry because of the witchcraft activity. She told me she noticed that spirit on me and she was always wondering if I were okay. I truly believe that as a result of me being in heavy intercession for that ministry and the main pastor, the demonic spirits transferred on me. I would ask myself, "How did I allow this to happen to me?" Although I knew that I was doing wrong, there was a drawing, a pushing, a pressing that kept me doing wrong. That spirit was in a lot of people in that church. So you see, the need to leave that ministry was a must. How can you get your deliverance where you'd gotten sick? When the head is sick, how can that body get well? It cannot! Although, this was not a pretty ending, it was good that I went through it because I can now write to you to tell you the story. Ask God today to sharpen your discernment. All of the pain that I endured allowed my spiritual eye to become wide open. I no longer take for granted the choices that I make in life. All of my decisions have to be tried through the fire. Will I get it wrong again? Yes, but being free from this circumstance will allow me to be less carefree and more reliant upon the Holy Ghost. That spell could only be broken in the spirit through a powerful prayer.

In conclusion, in the beginning, my recovery walk felt hopeless, dismal and dark; however, the first step to my recovery was instrumental — leaving that cult. Just leaving that place gave me such peace. My anxiety attacks and nightmares were still there; but as I pushed myself to pray and spend time with God, I began to see the light. For a while, I did not really communicate with anyone. All I wanted to do was sleep and cry. As I allowed God to continue healing and delivering me, I kept trusting Him and speaking His Word into existence over my life. I can say today that I have made the choice to surround myself with positive people and practice self-love. I am today an advocate for those experiencing narcissist abuse. My pain birthed my ministry – A Disciple for Christ. I am living today totally sold out for Him. If it were not for Yahweh who covered, protected and shielded me, I do not know where I would be. I can truly say that I am being made whole. I minister in the boldness of Christ Jesus, speaking the truth so that the lost can be set free. I will forever praise and lift His name. He has done great things for me.

I love the Lord and He truly heard my cry.

I am earnestly walking in the light.